HEDGEHOG IN YOUR GARDEN

DOREEN KING

Photographs: Doreen and Michael King
Illustrations: Graham Harding

ACKNOWLEDGEMENT

The author would like to thank Intervet UK Ltd for their generous support.

KINGDOM

CONTENTS

Designed by Add Graphics
PO Box 15
Waterlooville PO7 6BQ
England

Published by Kingdom Books
PO Box 15
Waterlooville PO7 6BQ
England

Kingdom Books is an
imprint of T.F.H. Publications

HEDGEHOG IN YOUR GARDEN

FOREWORD

from **Robin Squire**, MP

The hedgehog is a familiar visitor to many of our gardens and it is helpful to know how to provide assistance and care to this small creature. I have found Dr King's book both informative and interesting. It is written in an easy style and would provide any gardener or young person with the means of creating a 'hedgehog friendly' environment in their garden. There is an explanation on how to care for an undersized hedghog during the winter months or one that is sick or injured. Dr King encourages us to consider the wild creatures who share our gardens and makes us more aware of their needs. She has demonstrated how, by simple means, we can protect and encourage the hedgehogs in our garden.

Robin Squire, MP
House of Commons
1995

CHAPTER 1:

Introducing the HEDGEHOG

The hedgehog is unmistakable. This small but powerfully-built creature with the original 'spiky' hairstyle and the long, tapering snout is frequently seen at dusk and dawn, shuffling and snuffling determinedly around the edge of the garden in search of food. It is far from silent, emitting a bewildering range of hisses and snorts. Suburban residents have been woken up occasionally by the sounds of a hedgehog courtship ritual on their lawn, though these are not usually loud enough to disturb anyone. When the hedgehog is not in a hurry, it seems to move along as though it is on wheels, like a clock-work mouse, but if the need arises it can put on a fair turn of speed, its body lifting from the ground and its legs (at 10cm, comparatively long) clearly visible. Perhaps its best-known characteristic is that, when challenged or threatened by another animal, it immediately rolls itself into a tight ball, so that it is completely protected by the strong, sharp spines on its back and sides.

It might be helpful to begin by 'placing' the hedgehog within the animal world.

HEDGEHOG <u>IN YOUR GARDEN</u>

Since there are more than a million different species of animal on our planet, many of which resemble each other to a considerable extent, we need to be able to classify these species in an ordered, scientific way. The Swedish naturalist, Carolus Linnaeus, developed the Binomial System of Nomenclature for this purpose in the eighteenth century. According to this system, creatures are divided into **Classes**, one of which groups together creatures which suckle their young and is known as **Mammalia**, or **Mammals**. The Classes are then subdivided into Orders, and among the Mammals are such orders as **Carnivora** (meat-eaters like cats and dogs) and **Primates** (so-called 'highest' or 'prime' order, including monkeys, apes and man). Like shrews and moles, hedgehogs are mammals belonging to the order **Insectivora** (commonly called **Insectivores**), which indicates that their diet consists mainly of insects. In turn, the order Insectivora is subdivided into seven **Families** (*Erinaceidae* in the case of hedgehogs). These in turn are divided into **Genera** (singular: genus), which is *Erinaceus* for the hedgehog, and then again into **Species**. A species is defined by two names (hence the 'binomial system'), one indicating the genus and the other a specific name. The spiky visitor in our garden, then, is of the species *Erinaceus europaeus*, or Western (European) Hedgehog. Although different strains (varieties) are not usually associated with the European Hedgehog I have found that the colouring of individuals varies from chocolate to light brown or beige.

As its name suggests, the Western, or European, Hedgehog is found throughout Western Europe from southern Scandinavia in the north to the Mediterranean island of Sicily in the south. It is replaced by the Eastern Hedgehog (*Erinaceus concolor*) in Eastern Europe, the boundary being an imaginary line from the Adriatic Sea to the River Oder, which flows into the Baltic Sea opposite Sweden. Members of both species can be found within an area about 200km wide along this border.

The Eastern Hedgehog is similar to the Western Hedgehog, but distinguishable by being larger and having a lighter throat. The Algerian Hedgehog (*Erinaceus algirus*) originated in North Africa, as its name suggests, but is found also in the extreme south of Mediterranean Europe. It is smaller than the Western Hedgehog, with lighter underparts and larger ears. There is some disagreement about the total number of species of hedgehog but it is generally agreed that, looking further afield, there are two more species in Africa, two in China and a long-eared species, *Hemiechinus auritus*, in the deserts of the

HEDGEHOG <u>IN YOUR GARDEN</u>

Always examine new arrivals very carefully.

Middle East and India. Hedgehogs are not indigenous to the American continents, but interest in them has spread that far: the Four-toed, White-bellied or African Pygmy Hedgehog (*Erinaceus albiventris*) is growing in popularity as a pet in the USA. In the early twentieth century the Western Hedgehog was taken to New Zealand (for acclimatisation experiments, I understand) and it has become firmly and numerously established on both islands.

The Western Hedgehog is the only species of hedgehog found in Great Britain, and it is widely distributed throughout the country, though it does not like wet areas or barren, upland regions where there may be insufficient food and ground cover. It is very happy living in the gardens of suburbia, in close proximity to man. Hedgehogs are found even in central London, both in the parks and in small patio gardens and private conservatories. I have received calls about them from concerned residents. Sadly, many have perished on Central London roads.

In general, the hedgehog is very popular with human beings and many people put out food every night in the hope of enticing them into their gardens. This has not always been the case, however. The hedgehog was considered by many people to be vermin in the Middle Ages, and I understand that they were sometimes eaten, and still are. They are still unpopular with certain gamekeepers, as the eggs of small, ground-nesting birds sometimes provide snacks for hungry hedgehogs if they happen to find them.

Incidentally, the label 'insectivore' is possibly misleading when applied to a hedgehog. Hedgehogs are opportunists: as well as eating insects and such succulent delicacies as slugs and worms they enjoy seasonal fruits, and even small vertebrates such as frogs and shrews when they can surprise them. They will also raid domestic rubbish dumps and graciously accept any offerings of cat or dog food which people leave out. This is a much more suitable supplement to their diet than the traditional bread and milk, though that too will be greeted with enthusiasm.

The unusual characteristics of the hedgehog have caused various strange 'facts' to be associated with it. In his Natural History, the Roman writer Pliny claimed that hedgehogs carried berries to their nests by impaling them on their spines, though he does not mention how he thought they subsequently got them off to eat them! Apart from anything else, a hedgehog does not store food. It has also been claimed, wrongly, that hedgehogs are immune to the bite of the adder, the only venomous British snake. One could wonder whether the adder would not be more damaged in the attempt than the hedgehog, since its fangs are actually shorter than the hedgehog's spines. Hedgehog predators usually go for the surprise attack, aimed at the head and legs. There have also been tales of hedgehogs drinking milk from cows. Hedgehogs are opportunist feeders, and although they can climb, they do not like to do so. Furthermore, a kick from the cow could kill the hedgehog. However, a hedgehog may well enjoy a milk puddle from a leaking udder.

HEDGEHOG <u>IN YOUR GARDEN</u>

A garden hedgehog browsing on the lawn, though he is more interested in worms than grass.

Some of the tales told about hedgehogs are correct, however. They do have one or two peculiar habits. Of these, 'self-anointing' or 'foaming' is probably the strangest, and no-one can explain it satisfactorily. Certain hedgehogs will suddenly and for no apparent reason begin to lick themselves all over their backs and flanks, producing copious amounts of saliva and contorting themselves into the most peculiar shapes to spread it right across their spines. Then, after anything from one to ten minutes, they will stop and resume their previous activity as though nothing has happened. The stimulus for this behaviour can be provided by a variety of seemingly unconnected substances: toad skin, cigarette ends, furniture varnish or even plain distilled water. The confusion is compounded by the fact that it is not done by all hedgehogs when a substance is presented to them, and that those who do self-anoint may be of either sex. I have witnessed this behaviour in hedgehogs as young as three weeks old when they were presented with a new item of food. As saliva aids the absorption of smells it is highly likely that this behaviour is connected to the way in which the hedgehog learns about a new smell. Smell is most important to hedgehogs as they are nocturnal and have quite small eyes.

Hedgehogs have also often been observed running around in circles all on their own (nothing to do with the mating 'dance'). Some hedgehogs which have been brought in to me for this reason have had eye injuries, but others, on being examined by a vet, have been found to be well, with a normal sense of smell. As most of them were less than a year old, I suggest that they may have lost their way. Although hedgehogs are wanderers, they do like particular routes, so perhaps these ones were seeking for a trail or smell to follow, much as a bird

flies in circles to get its bearings. Such behaviour during the daytime would indicate illness, however.

Young hedgehogs are adorable creatures.

Because of the relatively small size and reclusive habits of the hedgehog it is very difficult to estimate its population in this country with any accuracy, although marking and radio tracking can record the movements of individual hedgehogs. The hedgehog is listed in Schedule VI of the Wildlife and Countryside Act of 1981, which affords it partial protection, stipulating that it may not be captured or killed by certain methods without a licence. (These methods are very narrowly and precisely described, and include the use of snares and explosive devices.) In January 1996 they were included under the Protection of Animals Act of 1911, which formerly required that an animal be deemed 'captive' for any act of cruelty against it to be an offence.

Although the hedgehog does not seem to be decreasing in this country, concern has been expressed for its survival in the wild in other parts of Europe. Because of its efficient defence mechanism it has few natural predators. However that very unnatural one, the motor car, is not intimidated by raised spines and the number of casualties on the roads remains sickeningly high. It is a good idea therefore to encourage the garden hedgehog, and to understand how to look after it when help is needed.

CHAPTER **2**: A **HEDGEHOG'S** life

Hedgehogs are inoffensive little creatures that are a delight to see in any garden. They live for about six years, sometimes as long as ten. Since they are nocturnal they will rarely be seen during the middle of the day; the best time for observing them is early in the morning or just as it is beginning to get dark.

HEDGEHOG IN YOUR GARDEN

Adult hedgehogs weigh about 800g on average, although their weight can approach 2kg. When they first emerge from hibernation, however, they weigh considerably less. As has already been stated, their backs and flanks are covered in spines which are about 2cm long. These are modified hairs, mostly cream in colour, with brown at the base, and a contrasting band, usually darker brown, just behind the point. Their faces, throats and undersides are clothed in longish, brown-grey fur. Hair is surprisingly sparse on their legs and tails.

The hedgehog's skin is rather loose and hangs down so that the fringe of hair along the bottom of the spiny part forms a 'skirt' as it walks along, hiding its legs and tail, and giving it the appearance of a toy on wheels. It is to this loose skin that the hedgehog owes its unique defence mechanism. There are special muscles below the surface of the skin which contract to pull it over the hedgehog's head and bottom. A circular muscle around the bottom of the skirt then contracts, acting like the string of an old-fashioned purse to pull the skin together to form a 'bag', with spikes on the outside and head, legs and tail tucked inside.

When a hedgehog responds to touch by immediately curling up into a tight ball, then you know that there is still plenty of life in it. If it is too weak to curl up, then it is in an extremely bad way.

Before rolling itself up completely into a ball the hedgehog will often react to a threat by hunching itself up, tucking its head in and moving forward menacingly, head-butting and hissing. When a hedgehog is young and inexperienced or has become too tame, it will often delay the full, defensive 'roll-up' too long, with disastrous results. As has already been stated, hedgehogs have few natural enemies as most are intimidated by the spikes. They do have some, however, and juveniles which have just left the nest are the most vulnerable. Badgers have a taste for hedgehogs, and will eat young and old alike; in fact, pieces of scattered hedgehog skin are an indication of the presence of badgers. Foxes will sometimes take infants still in the nest as well

Hedgehogs love to dig in the garden and they will ingest a lot of vegetation along with insects.

as juveniles. Hedgehogs are often injured by cats, and dogs can be a threat to hedgehogs. Humans also represent danger, and not only when driving cars. Few people eat hedgehogs in Great Britain nowadays, but hedgehogs are small enough to be victims of acts of horrifying cruelty. Attempts to prosecute have failed in the past because wild hedgehogs were not protected by the Protection of Animals Act until January 1996. More indirect injury from humans has resulted from the disappearance of hedgerows in the countryside, leading to a decrease in hedgehog breeding sites and protective habitat.

Hedgehogs are largely carnivorous but will eat a very wide range of food. They will vary their diet of invertebrates with berries and fruit but will also eat baby mice, baby birds, young frogs and toads, eggs - in fact, anything 'meaty' that is available, alive or dead. They have been known to try to eat quite large birds and animals, and have

HEDGEHOG IN YOUR GARDEN

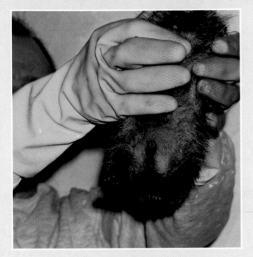

been condemned in the past for taking the eggs of large ground-nesting birds. They can crush pigeons' eggs if they come across them, but would have difficulty in breaking a hen's egg. They also tend to take in large quantities of leaves, grass and soil, which pass straight through them. Some travel a considerable distance every night in search of food, one or two miles not being uncommon.

Top left & middle:
A male hedgehog.
Bottom:
A female hedgehog.

The hedgehog sleeps during the day, either building a new nest or using one that has already been built. It has some homing instinct, sometimes returning to one particular nest every few days and sometimes using a nest once only. A ready-built nest might be used by more than one hedgehog, but never at the same time. Each hedgehog sleeps on its own: company is not appreciated. To build a nest it digs a trench under thick bushes and stones, lines it with grass and leaves and then adds the finishing touch by turning around and around to mould the nest with its prickles until it has a nice round cavity, thickly lined. The nests are extremely well camouflaged. On one occasion when I was sitting in my garden I was completely unaware that a hedgehog was sleeping barely a metre away until it woke up for a scratch!

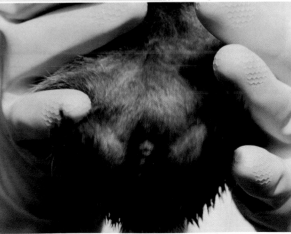

To sex a hedgehog, hold it upright. The male genitals are in the middle of its tummy. Female genitals are between the hind legs, near the tail.

15

CHAPTER **3**:

A HEDGEHOG-
friendly garden

Garden design

If you want to attract hedgehogs to your garden you must consider their likes and dislikes. Hedgehogs are wanderers by nature, so it is wrong to confine a hedgehog to one garden unless there is a good reason for doing so. A hedgehog will need at least 200 square metres of garden space if it is to forage successfully, and on farmland the norm is not more than one hedgehog to each 4000-8000 square metres. Furthermore, baby hedgehogs disperse as they become independent and need to find their own territories.

Hedgehogs, then, must be able to go in and out of the garden at will. If they cannot, they will be unable to find adequate food and shelter and you will have to feed them every day and provide bedding, shelter and water.

HEDGEHOG <u>IN YOUR GARDEN</u>

Hedgehogs hate to be disturbed in any way. For this reason they like parts of the garden which are not regularly cultivated, and they love thick, evergreen vegetation, with shrubs and climbers such as ivy. They enjoy foraging expeditions along the sides of hedges and walls and they like to sleep under sheds. However, they also enjoy closely-cut grass and one tell-tale sign of hedgehog activity is greenish droppings on your well-tended lawn. Another hedgehog attraction is the compost heap. Many a happy hedgehog family has been raised in the warmth generated by rotting compost.

Hedgehogs like parts of the garden that are not regularly cultivated.

Water and food in a garden will attract a wide range of wildlife, including hedgehogs. This should be taken into account when you consider the use of insecticides in the garden. Not only will insecticides deplete natural food supplies for hedgehogs, but they will also make them ill, possibly even killing them. It is worth noting also that some common plants such as foxgloves and lupins are poisonous, and hedgehogs (and children!) can become very ill if they eat them.

By all means plant your roses and beans, but also plant holly or some other evergreen shrubs. Eat your lettuces and

Whilst you are asleep there is a vast array of activity going on in your garden, and hedgehogs often come right up to back doors and around garden sheds in search of food.

blackberries, but leave a few for the garden residents. Keep your ornamental fish pond with your prize goldfish, but leave a wildlife pond for frogs and hedgehogs.

A gardener's aim is usually to make the garden as attractive and interesting as possible. What can enhance a beautiful, well-cultivated garden more than a wide selection of wildlife to watch? Of course, you will be likely to see the hedgehogs only at dawn and dusk, but a garden that attracts hedgehogs will certainly attract a variety of birds and butterflies as well.

Feeding hedgehogs

Hedgehogs have a keen sense of smell and eat a wide range of foods. When food is hard to find, particularly in cold autumn weather and in the middle of summer when the ground is hard, they will raid dustbins and eat whatever they can to survive. If you want to leave

food in the garden for your prickly friends you will be of the most help to them if you choose suitable foods.

A hedgehog released from a comfortable nest may decide to use it regularly.

Avoid giving your hedgehog biscuits or bread and cow's milk; remember that it is primarily a meat eater. It will enjoy most flavours of cat or dog food and also tinned fish such as sardines and pilchards. Studies involving the tracking of hedgehogs have indicated that they do not come to rely upon the food that humans put out for them, but treat it as a supplement to their natural diet, so you will not be too

Water can be a very attractive feature in a garden.

badly missed if you have to go away from home for a few days.

Put the food out just as it is getting dark. If there are hedgehogs around, it will not be there for long! Since food put out at night will attract less welcome visitors such as rats, foxes and cats, it is best to put it in a container which only

Wildlife ponds and drinking dishes may be used regularly by many different hedgehogs.

hedgehogs can reach easily. A rabbit hutch with a tunnel 5cm high by 10cm wide or a pipe of 12cm diameter, preferably with a sharp bend in it, leading to the door might be the answer. Plastic domestic waste disposal pipes are ideal. A simpler solution could be to put an upturned saucer over the food: a hedgehog can usually knock this off quite easily, but a cat cannot. Plants such as peppermint and catmint around the garden will help to discourage rodents.

Water

Water can be a very attractive feature in a garden, and hedgehogs are not the only creatures which will thank you for it. A water supply is vital to hedgehogs, particularly in the hot, dry summer months. The wildlife pond with gently sloping sides is most suitable, as traditional ornamental ponds with steep sides can be fatal. Hedgehogs can swim, but they may not be able to clamber out. As always, young hedgehogs just out of the nest are the most vulnerable. However, the ornamental pond can be made more hedgehog-friendly by adding flowerpots at the sides to form a ledge. The hedgehogs can then scramble up these to escape. Even a piece of chicken wire at each end would help, although this is far from ideal as their legs could get caught in it.

Ideally, swimming pools should be covered when not in use, as this is both safer and more hygienic. If your swimming pool has to be left uncovered, leave some pieces of wood floating on the water. Small creatures can then climb onto them and wait to be rescued. Needless to say, safety must also be a consideration where children are concerned. If there is no pond in your garden, an upturned dustbin lid or similar container can be filled with water and left at ground level to quench the thirst of your garden visitors. It should be cleaned out regularly.

Nesting sites

Hedgehogs like to make their nests around the overgrown perimeters of gardens. They need cover, and will nest against fences, under hedges, in dense vegetation and in piles of rubbish. Their great favourites are manure heaps and under sheds.

Be very careful when you are about to burn garden rubbish or fork over compost. Always look through it thoroughly first. A nesting hedgehog will usually move out on its own when the compost is disturbed, so you might consider looking over the compost and then leaving it for a while before working on it. If you uncover a female with babies, gently cover them up again and leave them alone, but keep your eyes and ears open. The mother may leave the young after she has been disturbed, and if the babies come out or you hear them crying they will need to be hand reared. (Their cry consists of quite loud, agitated squeaks, rather like that of a hungry guinea pig.) If the nest has been completely destroyed, again watch the mother and make sure that dogs and cats cannot get at the babies. She may take the young away, very possibly hiding by day and returning at dusk. Again, hand rearing will be necessary if she does not return. Always remember that hedgehogs hate to be disturbed.

Apart from the natural nesting sites in a hedgehog-friendly garden, why not make some 'purpose-built' ones available? Your hedgehog may consider an old bag of straw in the garden a most desirable residence, especially if it is buried, with an entrance pipe bent at a sharp angle and about 12cm in diameter. A rabbit hutch may be used if access to it is through a tunnel about 5cm high by 10cm wide (or preferably use a bent plastic waste-disposal pipe 12cm in diameter), but again it will probably be more acceptable if it is partly buried in the ground. An upturned canister with a hole in the side, buried in the ground so that it forms a hollow, may also be accepted.

Hedgehog-friendly gardening

When gardening, just think 'hedgehog' and you will not go far wrong so far as your prickly friend is concerned. Can the wire and netting you put down for your plants be kept about 12cm above the ground? If not, your resident hedgehog will sooner or later end up being trapped in the netting and wire. Its frantic efforts to get free can result in the most horrific injuries which are often aggravated by dirt, flies, and attacks by cats. The importance of examining manure heaps, compost heaps and piles of rubbish has already been stressed. The wise gardener will not leave hazardous rubbish such as odd bits of wire and netting and half-empty cans of paint or garden chemicals lying around. Like small children, hedgehogs will sample the most deadly poisons. They are also quite likely to enter the shed or garage when the door has been left ajar and step in the tray of paint which has been left on the floor, literally making their mark on the establishment.

The dangers of water to hedgehog and child alike have already been stressed. Drain holes should always be kept covered, as hedgehogs are very likely to fall down them. If you do find a hedgehog that is stuck down a drain, grip its spines with two pairs of pliers and pull

HEDGEHOG IN YOUR GARDEN

Hedgehogs like to forage freely on lawns, flower beds, and all over the garden.

hard. Hedgehogs are prone to falling down holes, so make sure that the garage inspection pit is covered, and provide a way out of cattle-grids.

Weed killers, insecticides and slug pellets can make hedgehogs ill, possibly killing them. Any substance which is likely to be harmful to birds and bees will probably harm hedgehogs too. Hedgehogs eat slugs and insects. Is it not better to protect this most organic of pest control agents rather than risk poisoning it?

There are obviously times when garden pests and weeds need to be controlled, particularly in the case of food crops. However, there are alternatives to chemicals. Refer to a good gardening book and you will find descriptions of age-old methods such as leaving a jar of beer to kill the slugs, or keeping them out by planting rows of chives around vegetable beds. Soapy water sprayed on roses will keep the greenfly away, and regular hoeing is preferable to regular spraying for weed control.

Friend or foe?

In the past hedgehogs have been persecuted by gamekeepers and conservationists alike because of their liking for the eggs and fledglings of ground-nesting birds. While this is a just accusation, it must also be recognised that they eat many other things as well. For example, they play a very efficient part in controlling the insect population. It is recognised by ecologists that balance in nature is essential, and that one link in the food chain cannot be destroyed without affecting the whole system. Gardeners have also complained about hedgehogs' calling cards left on their beautifully mown lawns. It is true that hedgehogs love to wander over closely clipped lawns and will leave droppings at random, but since the droppings are seldom longer than 4cm they can hardly be called a 'large' problem. In any case, the presence of hedgehogs will make a garden more interesting.

Families sometimes shun hedgehogs because they are regarded as 'flea-balls'. This is quite an accurate description as, like all wild animals, hedgehogs carry parasites. Unfortunately the hedgehog's 'passengers' are particularly noticeable because of its spines, which are sparse when compared with the dense fur coats of most animals. The fleas therefore have nowhere to hide. They are mostly host-specific fleas (fleas which only live on hedgehogs). Hedgehogs can also 'swap' fleas with the family cat or dog, but probably no more so than other wild animals. If you feel it is absolutely necessary to spray any hedgehogs you see in the garden, bird insecticides are extremely effective but mild and can, therefore, be used safely for this purpose. All family dogs and cats should be treated regularly for external parasites, as they are likely to pick them up now and then whether or not there are hedgehogs about.

Incidentally, the hedgehogs that have settled in New Zealand have no fleas, although they do have lice and ticks. Perhaps the fleas were not such good travellers as their hosts.

Hedgehog nests are extremely difficult to see. They are well camouflaged under bushes. They are sometimes easier to spot when the hedgehogs decide to use pieces of tissue paper and other coloured items which they have found on foraging trips.

CHAPTER 4:

Handling and housing HEDGEHOGS

Does your garden hedgehog need a helping hand?

You will usually be able to tell easily when your garden hedgehog needs a helping hand. Obviously, it will need to be freed if it has fallen down a hole or become tangled up in wire-netting. Not quite so obvious is the need to examine the hedgehog for 'fly strike'. This is most likely to have occurred if the hedgehog has been trapped during daytime, particularly in summer. Flies will seize the opportunity of laying their eggs on warm-blooded creatures that cannot move to protect themselves. If they are not removed, the eggs will hatch out into maggots, which will begin to eat the flesh of the unfortunate creature. This can result in death. Fly eggs are visible as clusters of tiny, white dots, and every single one of them must be removed from the affected hedgehog. (See Fly Strike in Chapter 5.)

HEDGEHOG IN YOUR GARDEN

Something is usually very wrong if a hedgehog is found wandering during the day and you should not release it unless you are quite sure there is no physical problem. If it is found in November and weighs less than 450g, it should be taken into care even if it is not sick or injured. It can be released in a mild spell once it has reached 500g, but it is better to keep it till

A young hedgehog.

spring. Any hedgehog found crying, wobbling or shivering will need assistance.

Remember, too, that hedgehogs breed from May to September, so if a female is taken into care during this period it could lead to the death of her litter. It is extremely difficult to determine whether a female is pregnant or lactating.

If a hedgehog is disturbed while sleeping during the daytime it may leave its nest and look for a new place to sleep. Again, be watchful for babies if you know that this has happened. Baby hedgehogs, or hoglets, are whitish brown at one to two weeks, becoming brown and weighing about 200g by four weeks. They can sometimes be found wandering if their mother has not returned to the nest and, in this case, will need to be taken into care. If you hear babies calling continuously from their nest during the day (quite loud, high-pitched squeaks, rather like those of a guinea pig) this is probably an indication that their mother has not returned from a foraging trip, so they will need help. If you find one baby hedgehog in distress, always look for more. There are usually more than two babies in a litter.

Do take care, however, to assess the situation thoroughly. I received a call one morning from a woman who had found three tiny hoglets in the middle of her lawn, one of which was dead. The female hedgehog had apparently been disturbed at her nest, or had decided that it was no longer suitable. Just as she was in the process of

Coloured beads are especially useful for identification.

HEDGEHOG IN YOUR GARDEN

Young hedgehogs can usually be examined easily as they are not afraid to unroll.

moving her week-old babies the woman had unwittingly gone into the garden and frightened her. A cage was put over the surviving babies and they were kept warm. That night, at dusk, their mother returned to collect them.

To summarise, then: if a nest has been destroyed and the mother is killed or deserts it, the babies will need to be collected and taken into care. If the nest has been accidentally disturbed, cover it immediately and keep a close eye on it. Even if the mother leaves it initially, she may return.

Always wear gloves when handling a hedgehog for the first time.

Handling

Before attempting to handle a hedgehog, spray it with a bird insecticide outdoors and allow about 15 minutes for the insects to drop off. Then put on gloves and check for ticks and any other external parasites. (See **Parasites** in Chapter 5.)

Always wear gloves when handling a hedgehog for the first time. Heavy duty plastic gloves are useful for picking up large, adult hedgehogs, and gloves should always be used if disease or ringworm is suspected. Heavy duty plastic gloves can be disinfected and re-used. When lifting a hedgehog, slip your fingers underneath it to avoid the spines. If you are going to handle hedgehogs regularly check that your tetanus inoculations are up to date. Hedgehogs do not normally bite, but a sick one may. The bite is very weak, however, and will not usually break the skin.

If you find a hedgehog and need to take it to a vet or carer but are concerned about handling it, then don't. Just sweep it gently into a box.

Hedgehogs generally like to dig downwards and some may prefer to sleep under hutches rather than in them. However, there is no accounting for taste and one particular hedgehog liked to sleep in my brother's tortoise hutch. Hutches tend to be sold with swivel latches and these can easily be opened by cats and foxes. Bolts should always be used.

Housing

When housing hedgehogs together you will need to be able to identify them. This can easily be done by putting a bead onto a spine with a dab of glue. You can cut off the spine before release if you want to. It is normal for hedgehogs to build nests even when they are very young. They will tear up tissue and newspaper to make what is, to us, a real mess and, to them, a very nice nest. Hedgehogs kept together will be particularly likely to 'foam' or 'self-anoint'. This process has already been described in Chapter 1: Introducing the hedgehog. The hedgehog produces an enormous amount of saliva and licks itself (and sometimes other hedgehogs too) all over. No-one knows quite why they do this, but it is usually triggered by new smells.

Housing baby hedgehogs

Baby hedgehogs less than two weeks old should be kept in incubators or over heating pads (lowest setting) at a constant temperature of about 30°C. Plastic containers about 60cm by 30cm are suitable, lined with newspaper and tissue. The hoglets should be given a plastic teddy as a comforter and covered loosely with tissue, rags and bubble film. At about two weeks old (100g weight), when they can curl up, they can be kept at a constant room temperature of about 21°C in their plastic containers.

At two to three weeks old (150g weight) they can be transferred in their boxes to an unheated room. As the hoglets become more mobile it is a good idea to divide the container into two parts, one with the nesting material in it to be the more sleeping compartment, and the other just lined with newspaper where the food and water bowls can be placed. This will help to keep the sleeping area clean and dry.

At three to four weeks old, provided they are fully weaned, the hoglets can be transferred to outdoor rabbit hutches. Line the rabbit hutch with newspaper and put hay in the sleeping quarters. Wood shavings can be sprinkled in the other section.

Housing adult hedgehogs

Sick hedgehogs should be kept at a constant room temperature of 21°C. Hot water bottles, lamps and heating pads are not necessary if the room is kept warm. Hedgehogs can quickly become overheated and a sick hedgehog may not be able to move to a cooler position. Use a lamp or heating pad only if the animal is cold to the touch. Put the hedgehog in a plastic box lined with newspaper and plenty of tissue. If possible divide the container into two parts, so that one part can be used as the sleeping compartment. I use plastic storage boxes with a small carton for the sleeping quarters. It may be necessary to put netting over the tops of the boxes if your guests are ardent climbers, as hedgehogs can easily get out of containers up to 15cm high.

HEDGEHOG IN YOUR GARDEN

House hedgehogs separately wherever possible. As has already been said, they do like to sleep alone. Females should always be housed separately in case they are pregnant as the new-born hoglets could be eaten by the other hedgehogs. Injured hedgehogs should also be housed separately, as hedgehogs sometimes bite injured limbs - on occasions even their own! Some hedgehogs are particularly active at night. They are natural diggers and may end up with injured feet if they are kept for any length of time in plastic boxes. Transfer them outside to rabbit hutches as soon as possible.

However great the temptation, hedgehogs that are to be released should be handled as little as possible.

Transfer hedgehogs outside as soon as possible.

Transfer the hedgehogs in their boxes to an unheated room for a few days as soon as they show signs of recovery. They can then be housed outdoors in individual rabbit hutches. Line the hutches with newspaper and put hay in the sleeping quarters. Sprinkle wood shavings in the other section. However, do not use woodshavings, hay or cat litter for the housing of hedgehogs with open wounds or for those recovering from surgery. Such hedgehogs must be kept on tissue or preferably absorbent paper towels.

If you need to keep a hedgehog for a long time, fit a closed run to the hutch if possible, but remember that the enclosing material must be secured at ground level, preferably extending below the ground. Hedgehogs are ardent diggers - as are their natural enemies such as cats, dogs, foxes and badgers. It is best to enclose the run with wire, the wire at the bottom being covered with earth. Most rabbit hutches are supplied with swivel lever locks. I always add a bolt because some cats and foxes can push a lever down with their paws. For the sake of the birds do not house hedgehogs in aviaries, as they may bite the legs of small ground birds and eat eggs and chicks.

Many hedgehogs will stay awake during the winter if they are fed daily and housed in sheds or outdoor rabbit hutches. If the weather gets really cold, however, the hedgehogs may hibernate. Do not allow a sick hedgehog or a hedgehog weighing less than 450g to do so. They will not usually try to hibernate unless they are well above this weight. If one shows signs of doing so, keep it at 21°C until its weight increases and then gradually acclimatise it by lowering the temperature by a few degrees daily.

All captive hedgehogs should be examined regularly for signs of disease. They should also be treated with insecticide and wormed regularly. (See **Parasites** in Chapter 5.) Nursing mothers will tolerate a peep to see if they are all right.

Toe clipping

If a hedgehog needs to be kept in a plastic box for a long time the enforced inactivity might cause its toe nails to grow abnormally long. This should rectify itself once the hedgehog is transferred to an outside pen, but sometimes the nails might need to be trimmed.

First, unroll your hedgehog! (See Chapter 5 for hints on this.) Then hold its claws up to a light and note where the blood vessels end. You will see this by the change in colour, the nail becoming lighter and translucent when it is 'dead'. Finally, clip the nails with heavy duty clippers, starting well away from the blood vessels.

HEDGEHOG IN YOUR GARDEN

Transport

Always transport hedgehogs in small containers so that they cannot roll around. They are usually quite happy to sleep through long journeys if they are transported in small boxes lined with plenty of tissue. Avoid transporting hedgehogs at night, when they will be more lively.

Grace King with one of the hedgehogs which she was hand-rearing.

CHAPTER 5

Treating
HEDGEHOGS

Introduction to treatment

Before examining a hedgehog it is best to get rid of the parasites (see **Parasites** on Page 53.)

In my experience there are two main groups of hedgehogs needing care: babies in difficulties and juveniles with injuries. In the case of the juveniles the usual problem is a bite from a fox, cat, dog or some

If you see a hedgehog out during the day time do take it out of reach of flies. This hedgehog had leg injuries and had been seen during daylight over a period of three days. It had advanced fly strike. One leg had to be amputated.

HEDGEHOG IN YOUR GARDEN

other predator when the hedgehog has been slow to roll up. The result is an injury to face or limbs which is aggravated by dirt and fly strike as the hedgehog goes on its way. Limbs often need to be amputated, but I can assure you that a hedgehog can still run with only one back leg.

It is important to examine a hedgehog very carefully, especially for fly strike (clusters of tiny white dots). Unless the hedgehog is very young, it should be rolled up tightly. If it is not, it is obviously very poorly and needs immediate attention.

Look carefully all over the hedgehog's back, gently parting the spines with a pencil to examine for cuts and fly strike. Turn the hedgehog over (even if it is a ball!) and examine all accessible parts. Cuts and fly strike can easily be missed. Examine the legs, head and belly. Pay particular attention to the nose and mouth, as injuries to these parts are common. Examine the eyes and ears.

If there are obvious breaks to the limbs, put the hedgehog into a small box to restrict its movement until the vet can deal with the injuries. If there are not, put it down and observe the way it moves. Is it dragging a leg? Is it reluctant to move at all? (Bear in mind that you may have to wait a long time for a healthy hedgehog to uncurl.)

If the hedgehog is curled into a tight ball you probably will not be able to examine its underparts. Young hedgehogs can sometimes be induced to unroll by being held either belly side up or belly side down, tipping the front end backwards and forwards. As soon as the hedgehog begins to unroll, slip your fingers onto the belly and hold the hedgehog 'open'. If you really need to unroll a stubborn hedgehog, dip it into a bowl of tepid water and, as it uncurls, slide a hand across its abdomen with the thumb gently pressing down on its back to prevent it from rolling up again. If you have trouble unrolling the hedgehog, and injury is suspected, the vet may decide to anaesthetize it to see what is wrong. This must be done as soon as possible in case its wounds are infected with maggots. It is always wise to have a hedgehog checked by a vet if there is any doubt about its well-being.

After the examination, the hedgehog should be weighed. (It should subsequently be weighed once a week during its captivity.) Next, it can be fed, unless it is an adult which is going to be treated by a vet that day. It should be noted that hedgehogs sometimes go off their food for several days after being given antibiotics.

Hedgehogs are often brought in with head injuries.

HEDGEHOG IN YOUR GARDEN

Hedgehogs often bite and chew their injuries, particularly cuts on limbs. Covering the limbs with plastic hair curlers or the cardboard tubes inside toilet rolls can be useful. As has already been stated, it is best to isolate injured hedgehogs.

Remember that any baby hedgehog taken into care will need toileting (see Chapter 6). This is a very simple process, but the animal will die if it is not done.

Hedgehogs that do not attempt to curl up when you examine them are very ill indeed.

Homeopathy

The word 'homeopathy' means the treatment of disease by using small amounts of a drug that, in healthy persons, produces symptoms similar to those being treated.

It is best to consider all available treatments and to start with those known to have been successful in the past. The course of treatment should always be discussed fully with a vet. The following homoeopathic preparations have been found helpful by some carers in treating hedgehogs:

Aconite - for shock.
Arnica - for traumatised animals.
Calcarea phosphorica - for the healing of broken bones.
Calendula - for open wounds.
Carbo-vegitabilis - for the revival of 'almost dead' hedgehogs.
Hepar-sulph - for the healing of abscesses.
Hypericum - for pain relief after surgery. On no account should this be used instead of an anaesthetic.
Silicea - for pellet wounds (use for one day only).

Homeopathic remedies generally come in the form of tablets, the usual dosage being one tablet of 200 strength daily. The tablet can be crushed and added to the hedgehog's food. Creams and lotions should be applied generously according to instructions.

Quick guide to problems

(For full details, refer to **Alphabetical list of common ailments and their treatments.**)

Bald patches: Suspect ringworm or mange mites. Isolate. However, I have also found that bald, flaky patches may result from poor condition. A daily teaspoon of sterile bonemeal and a generous pinch of vitamin powder (both available from pet shops) on the food may rectify the condition within a matter of days.

Broken bones: Seek veterinary assistance.

Burns: Apply cold water immediately.

Cold to the touch (especially the belly): Warm slowly (no direct heat).

Coughing and/or going light: Suspect worms or possibly disease. Isolate. ('Going light' is a phrase often used about birds as well as hedgehogs to describe rapid loss of weight not connected with diet. They may also feel limp and 'floppy' when you pick them up.)

Eggs and/or maggots: Fly strike (*myiasis*). Treat immediately.

Underweight: Do not release a hedgehog in the summer until it weighs about 350g. If it is under 450g in November it should not be released until the following spring.

Watery eyes and/or discharge from mouth and/or nose and diarrhoea: Suspect disease. Isolate and seek veterinary assistance.

Wheezing: Hedgehogs are susceptible to pneumonia when they are injured and cannot find warm, dry cover. Therefore suspect pneumonia and seek veterinary advice.

Wobbling/Shivering/Cold to the touch: Suspect dehydration. Immediately offer goat's milk (or milk formulated for kittens or puppies), water and raw minced meat. Warm hedgehog slowly.

HEDGEHOG IN YOUR GARDEN

Examine the eyes, ears, nose and mouth. Then examine the belly, each foot in turn, and the tail.

It is advisable to ask your vet to look at the hedgehog, especially if it is badly injured or looks as if it is diseased. Most hedgehog casualties have some degree of dehydration, so it is important to observe the hedgehog's food and drink intake on the day of arrival and throughout captivity, and treat for this condition if necessary.

If you feel unable to nurse the hedgehog yourself your local directory or vet may be able to furnish you with the name of a contact who will nurse it for you. If you do decide to nurse it yourself this contact might be able to offer advice.

If you take a hedgehog to the vet do explain that, if it does stand some chance of recovery, you are willing to nurse it or know someone who is. Otherwise the vet might think you want the hedgehog put to sleep.

Alphabetical list of common ailments and their treatments

Air sacs: Air sacs under the skin may be caused by injuries leading to infection. The skirt (fringe of hair around the belly) might be drawn up by the pressure of an air sac with the result that the hedgehog cannot roll up and is therefore helpless. Your vet can draw off the air with a sterile syringe. If the air sac reappears an antibiotic might be necessary.

Broken bones/torn and displaced muscles/dislocations: It is advisable to seek veterinary assistance as soon as possible. Broken bones will need to be set, and dislocated bones and displaced muscles will need to be manipulated under anaesthetic. The back muscles can be displaced so that the tail is pulled up over the back. These muscles can be manipulated successfully under anaesthetic.

Allow four weeks for bad breaks to heal. After a splint is removed it might be a few more weeks before the limb is fully functional. When there is a broken pelvis the animal might need assistance in emptying the bladder. If this is the case, gently squeeze the abdomen. Suspect a broken pelvis if the animal is having difficulty in moving both the back legs. There are differing views as to whether a female should be released after suffering a broken pelvis because of the possibility of problems if she subsequently becomes pregnant.

The following conditions might all result in the hedgehog not being able to move its rear end: two broken legs, a broken pelvis, a broken back, or displaced muscles. However, the loss of mobility could also be due to internal injury or vitamin deficiency. Each animal must be

Hedgehogs often sustain head injuries when they are attacked and do not curl up quickly enough. They can look very severe yet be mostly superficial. Large scabs are visible on this hedgehog and once they drop off the wounds tend to heal quickly.

assessed individually. Vitamins (such a teaspoonful of SA37 daily) added to the food would be beneficial in all cases.

Sadly, it may be best to have a hedgehog with a broken pelvis put to sleep. Your vet will advise. Also, broken limbs are often impossible to set because of movement of the bones and infection of the tissues. Provided the infection has not reached into the pelvic cavity, amputation might be possible. Euthanasia would usually be considered if an animal would only have one front leg or if there was a problem with both back legs. A hedgehog with only one front leg could make a nice pet, but it is uncertain if it could survive in the wild as hedgehogs need to dig for food.

Burns: Hedgehogs are very susceptible to

Raw mince is a favourite. They are also extremely fond of sultanas.

burns, particularly around Bonfire Night, as they like nothing better than to tuck themselves up into nice piles of garden refuse.

Apply cold water immediately to cool down the tissues. Give the hedgehog plenty to drink and seek veterinary assistance. If the burns result in broken skin, follow the treatment for cuts. Fluid therapy is advisable if there is substantial loss of skin (see section on **Dehydration**).

Cold/wet hedgehogs and dying hedgehogs: Note that a wet hedgehog might not necessarily be cold! Cold/wet hedgehogs and dying hedgehogs are usually reluctant to move. Breathing may be rapid or irregular and the animal may moan. Sometimes breathing is too shallow to be detected and the animal might appear to be dead. As with any animal, do not give up on it until it goes stiff. If the legs and belly feel cold to the touch even after the hedgehog has been left for a while in a warm room then warm it slowly, using a heating pad, heating lamp or incubator. Take it off the heat source once the belly and legs feel warm to the touch and see the section on **Housing** in Chapter 4. Offer it a bowl of goat's milk (or kitten or puppy formula) and a bowl of raw minced meat.

If the hedgehog is well enough to swallow, give it a carbo-vegitabilis tablet and force feed 3-5ml goat's milk (see section on Force Feeding in chapter 6). Keep it warm and check after one hour. If there is no improvement give it a further 3-5ml goat's milk and a tablet of Arnica. Continue giving it goat's milk hourly until it shows signs of recovery. Then offer it a bowl of milk and a bowl of raw minced meat.

If the hedgehog is unconscious, your vet might be able to give it a rehydration injection, which sometimes helps (see **Dehydration**).

Cuts and bites: All cuts and bites should be disinfected daily for at least five days. A

Clusters of tiny white dots (fly eggs) are not always easy to see, but every one of them must be removed.

standard veterinary disinfectant for cuts is best, but if this is not available, any disinfectant designed for humans can be applied, following the instructions for use on children. Cuts on the nose, as well as the

Ticks may be found on any part of a hedgehog and they are often hidden behind the ears and limbs.

back, are common. Old infected cuts will need careful attention. If there is a very bad infection you might be able to smell the rotting tissue. Bathe such cuts daily with salt water. Animals suffering from severely infected wounds are usually given a course of antibiotic treatment by the vet (usually Penicillin). Cuts heal best when they are kept very dry, so a powder wound dressing should be applied daily. These are available from veterinary practices, and are also very useful for fly strike. Inspect for eggs and maggots twice or three times a day for the first three days. Take care that the smallest cut is not overlooked as fly strike can be fatal.

Deep cuts exposing internal organs will need suturing. As has already been said, an animal with cuts on its limbs should be isolated in case the others attack it.

Dehydration: Wobbling, shivering or helpless hedgehogs found wandering during the day should be treated for dehydration. They usually respond poorly to touch and may not even attempt to roll up. The skin of the back may be loose and you may be able to pull the spines and pinch up the skin. With healthy hedgehogs you should not be able to pull up the skin of the back. Keep a hedgehog in this condition warm (see Chapter 4) and immediately offer it a bowl of goat's milk or milk formulated for puppies or kittens. If it drinks this, give it a bowl of raw minced meat about half an hour later. The treatment is similar to that for cold hedgehogs.

If the hedgehog is fully conscious and warm to the touch (cold hedgehogs may not feed) but still refuses the milk, force feed 3-5ml goat's milk (see Chapter 6). If the hedgehog is not fully conscious your vet may be able to give it a rehydration injection, or a course of them if necessary. If all goes smoothly, the hedgehog should stop shaking and begin to behave normally after about an hour. It is best to keep such hedgehogs for a couple of days and to give them large quantities of milk and water to drink. If she is a female and there is any possibility that she has a family you should consider releasing her as soon as she begins to behave normally. Bear in mind, however, that as a dehydrated hedgehog has usually been in very poor condition for days it is unlikely that such a female will have a live litter.

Diseases: Hedgehogs can carry salmonella and leptospirosis organisms (which cause Weil's disease in humans). They can also carry avian tuberculosis, leprosy and rabies (though not, of course, in Great Britain). I must stress that I do not know of any case of such a disease being transmitted from hedgehog to human, but it remains a possibility. There is a slightly higher risk of infection from the parasites that hedgehogs carry (see **Parasites**).

Isolate the hedgehog and seek veterinary advice if it has any of the following symptoms:

Hedgehogs must be examined thoroughly. Time is needed to look at them very carefully.

- Discharge from the ears and/or mouth and/or nose.
- Disorientation and/or head held sideways and/or dull eyes.
- Pussy or watery eyes.
- Scabs, rashes or lesions.
- Sickness and/or diarrhoea.
- Sneezing and/or wheezing.
- Swollen eyes and/or joints.

The external signs of many diseases are non-specific and the cause cannot usually be identified fully without laboratory tests. The vet will probably prescribe antibiotics, the usual method being by injection into the muscles on the side of the back.

Unnatural behaviour is normally the first sign of illness. Hedgehogs will often show signs of distress if they are ill. They might groan. Blood in the stools (especially of baby hedgehogs) might indicate coccidia infection. In this case consult a vet. Hand-reared hedgehogs seem to be particularly prone to infection at the weaning stage. The use of a probiotic prior to weaning may be useful. This is a treatment which promotes the development of 'defensive' behaviour in the animal's immune system, and it can be bought at your pet shop. Hedgehogs may be seen with a 'blown up' belly. Gas-forming bacteria multiplying in the stomach and intestine may be responsible. If there are air sacs or fluid sacs under the skin which are preventing the hedgehog from moving, your vet may draw the air or fluid away using a syringe.

Ears: Always inspect ears for maggots, eggs and mites. Flush out maggots with warm water and pick out eggs with tweezers (see **Fly strike**). If mites are suspected fill the ear with cooking oil and swab daily.

Eyes: If a hedgehog runs in circles, check for blindness. The eyes may be shut due to injury, dirt or infection. Bathe them hourly in warm water for a few hours, and if they do not open try to ease the lids apart gently. Consult a vet if the eyes are injured or infected and bathe them several times a day with warm water. Bites to the head often result in substantial swelling and therefore closure of the eyes. The situation usually rectifies itself as the wounds heal, but wait until the eyes are fully open before release. Bear in mind also that hedgehogs with chest complaints or colds may have their eyes closed.

Always inspect eyes for maggots, eggs and mites. Maggots and eggs must be removed either with tweezers or by flushing out with warm water (see **Fly strike**). A one-eyed hedgehog should be able to cope in the wild.

Fly strike (myiasis): As has already been stated, fly strike occurs when a fly lays its eggs on a hedgehog. This usually happens when the hedgehog has been trapped outside in the daytime, particularly in hot weather. The resultant maggot infestation is common in hedgehogs, and fly strike is usually fatal if it is not treated quickly. If a hedgehog has been out during the day fly strike should always be suspected.

Check open wounds and cuts every few hours for signs of eggs and maggots. The eggs are visible as tiny white dots. They are easy to miss, but every one must be removed. Then check the whole body, parting spines gently with a pencil to examine the skin. The eyes, ears and mouth should be checked particularly carefully. Flush out maggots with warm water and pick out the eggs and remaining maggots with tweezers. A warm hair dryer can be used to dry cuts and make the maggots come to the surface, and it can be applied to the ear for the same purpose. Your vet may be able to supply a suitable cream or powder to help kill any remaining maggots in open wounds. A little talc can be applied (though not to open wounds) if eggs have been found. This will help to keep the hedgehog dry and prevent any remaining eggs from hatching.

Hibernation: This is a perfectly normal process for hedgehogs, but it is mentioned here because hedgehogs are often disturbed in hibernation by being dug out of their nests by animals or even by gardeners. Since it sometimes takes four or five hours for the hedgehog's temperature to return to normal, it can be picked up while still comatose in the belief that it is sick or because it is in a dangerous place. If it weighs more than 450g, and the weather is reasonably mild, it can be released in a suitable location, preferably surrounded by suitable material for nest building, and with food available.

Labour: Female hedgehogs can be pregnant at any time from May to September, and injuries and stress could induce early labour. The hedgehog in labour is very sluggish, and will probably be medium to large in size (800g or more). Her tummy will feel soft and lumpy, she may look a little pear-shaped and she will be reluctant to curl up. If labour is suspected, isolate the hedgehog immediately and ensure that she is given a place of her own where she will not be disturbed.

Oiled hedgehogs: Many people keep oil in their garages and hedgehogs sometimes have mishaps with trays of oil left lying around. If you find an 'oiled hedgehog', remove tar and grease with a hand cleaner such as Swarfega, available from a hardware store. Wash the hedgehog in washing-up liquid as soon as possible. (Some brands are better than others for this purpose and I have found that Co-op and Fairy are both suitable.) The water should be about 45°C, and you should have two buckets of hand-hot, soapy water and one bucket of warm rinsing water. Immerse the hedgehog up to its neck. The oil can be washed off its back with a soft brush, and its head can be gently cleaned with a toothbrush. Tip heavily soiled water away and repeat the process. Rinse the hedgehog thoroughly, mop off the excess water and put it near a heater to dry. If the animal has obviously swallowed oil and is extremely poorly, the usual treatment is about 4ml kaolin (available from your vet) followed by fluid therapy (see **Poisons**) and one teaspoonful of medicinal liquid paraffin daily for two days given on its food.

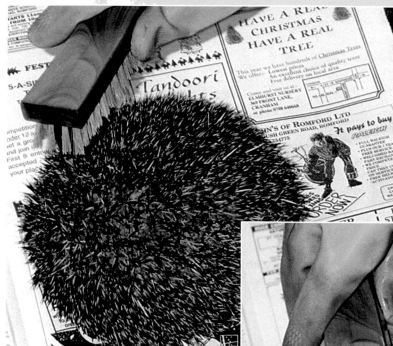

Parasites: Parasites are found on (external parasites) and in (internal parasites) healthy hedgehogs and are usually only a problem when the animal's resistance is low and the number of parasites increases excessively. They can be grouped as follows:

External parasites: Mites, ticks, lice, fleas, flies.

This hedgehog had severe ringworm. A weekly grooming ensured that infectious material was removed and new spines grew.

Internal parasites: Worms (including roundworms, tapeworms, flukes and spiny-headed worms). Other organisms.

If a hedgehog is taken into care, the removal of **external parasites** is a 'must' for reasons of hygiene. However, since hedgehogs usually carry a large number of external parasites, there is an argument for leaving them alone if the hedgehog is to be released immediately. This is because as soon as it is released it will begin to pick up new parasites but, if there is no controlling 'resident' population, whatever it picks up could multiply excessively, causing the hedgehog to become weakened. There is little evidence to support this view, but it remains a possibility.

It is important to avoid handling hedgehogs with external parasites with bare hands. Wear stout gloves, and avoid being bitten. Never touch external parasites. As well as being host to a great number of fleas, hedgehogs usually carry ticks and mites. Biting insects can cause disease to humans. Ticks can cause Lyme disease (Borrelia burgdorferi) and mites can cause scabies. Hedgehogs which are to be kept captive should, therefore, be sprayed with a bird insecticide on arrival, and this should be repeated as necessary.

Ticks: Remove by dabbing with cooking oil or surgical spirit, wait about 15 minutes for them to die and then remove them with tweezers. A more effective method is to apply an insect spray (for birds, cats and dogs) to a piece of cotton wool, and then to dab the tick with this. It should then fall off. If the animal is heavily infected with ticks, consult your vet, who may give it an injection to control the infestation. It is worth noting, should the worst happen, that however stubborn a tick has been about leaving its host while the hedgehog is still alive it will go in search of new food and lodging within half an hour of its death. If the hedgehog dies despite your efforts on its behalf its sleeping quarters should therefore be cleaned and disinfected very carefully.

Mites: Not a problem in small numbers, but in large numbers they can cause mange, so that the spines fall out and the skin becomes crusty. Since mites can live in the hollow shafts of the spines, it is difficult to remove them by spraying. The whole hedgehog (except for the head!) may need to be dipped in a mild insecticide. Consult a vet; as with ticks, your vet may decide to inject the animal to control the infestation. Cooking oil can be applied to the hedgehog's back if the skin is very crusty. Damaged spines can be brushed out, using a soft brush, and your vet may supply ear drops if the ears are also infested.

Suspect **internal parasites** if the hedgehog is coughing and/or 'going light'. Consult a vet: they are usually easy to treat. Hedgehogs kept on a long term basis should be de-wormed regularly. Usually a cat wormer available from your pet shop is used.

Poisoning: Any sudden large-scale death of hedgehogs should be reported and poisoning suspected.

The usual treatment for poisoning is 4ml of a product containing kaolin. Your vet will be able to supply this and advise about the dose. This is followed by plenty of fluids (goat's milk is suitable) for a couple of days. However, if you know what poison your hedgehog has eaten, your vet may consider administering a specific antidote.

Ringworm: Ringworm is caused by a fungus. Most types of fungus causing ringworm glow under ultra-violet light but *Trichophyton erinacei* (the hedgehog ringworm fungus) is one which does not fluoresce. The spines fall out and the skin becomes 'dandruffy'. Consult a vet, as this can usually be treated successfully. Ringworm can be stubborn and may take 12 weeks or more to clear up completely, especially if it is severe. Infected spines can be brushed out using a soft brush. If all else fails, the condition can be eased by applying an athletes' foot powder. Ringworm is very contagious, and hedgehog ringworm can easily be transmitted to humans. This is a major reason why gloves should be worn when handling infected hedgehogs.

Note that loss of spines is also a symptom of mite infestation or vitamin deficiency.

HEDGEHOG IN YOUR GARDEN

A hedgehog needs a healthy coat of spines for protection.

CHAPTER 6:

Feeding captive HEDGEHOGS

Hedgehogs are usually easy to feed once you know what they like. Cat food is probably best, but dog food too can be used. Some hedgehogs will turn up their noses at most of the flavours and brands of pet food you offer, but one or two types should suit - usually the most expensive! Hedgehogs have good appetites, and can happily account for a large (400g) tin of cat or dog food a day. As a general guide, a large hedgehog can eat as much as a cat.

It is best to offer a variety of foods. Most hedgehogs will accept raw minced meat, but it is advisable to add half a teaspoonful of vitamin supplement daily if it will eat nothing else. SA37 is suitable, and available from most pet shops. Occasionally a hedgehog which has been eating well will suddenly go off its food. This could be due to illness, but it is just as likely to be because it is finicky, and a change of dog or cat food could solve the problem. It is important to watch its diet closely.

HEDGEHOG IN YOUR GARDEN

Apart from meat, hedgehogs will accept mealworms, tinned fish and proprietary insect-based foods. They like unroasted peanuts, are very fond of sultanas and dried fruit and will accept small quantities of fresh fruit. They will also eat insect food for birds (Mynah bird food, for example). It is possible to buy food specially formulated for hedgehogs, one supplier being C J Wildbird Foods Ltd (see

In the wild, hedgehogs travel long distances in search of food.

Useful Addresses). Always give your hedgehog a bowl of clean water every night. Dishes for food and drink should be heavy-duty, non-tip dog or cat bowls. Some hedgehogs will still manage to tip up their bowls every night. Large bowls for water are therefore not a good idea as they can result in very wet hedgehogs.

Force feeding

Occasionally it might be necessary to force feed a hedgehog. The following method can only be used if the hedgehog is conscious and able to swallow.

Hedgehogs will happily feed together when dishes of food are provided for them.

Occasionally it is necessary to force feed a hedgehog.

HEDGEHOG IN YOUR GARDEN

Use a syringe with a small piece of rubber tubing fitted to the end. Support the hedgehog upright on its hind legs and gently force the syringe into its mouth. To do this you will have to open its mouth. Hedgehogs have a relatively weak bite, so the mouth can usually be forced open easily. A tube can be slipped down the throat if necessary. Be careful not to damage the hedgehog's teeth, and do avoid being bitten. As has been said before, anyone regularly handling hedgehogs should keep their tetanus inoculations up to date.

Goat's milk is adequate for hedgehogs more than two weeks

Hedgehogs aged about four weeks should start to eat and drink from dishes. They like goat's milk and this can be offered in a dish.

old, but see Chapter 7 for hand rearing baby hedgehogs. Drip the milk onto the hedgehog's tongue and watch it swallow. It should lap up the milk as you drip it, but take care not to drip it too quickly. If the hedgehog begins to cough, stop immediately. After feeding, wipe away any milk that has run down its belly.

CHAPTER 7 :

Hand rearing baby HEDGEHOGS

Pinkies (hedgehogs up to two weeks old) are best kept in incubators or on heating pads at about 30°C. At this stage, the hoglets are pink with soft, white-brown spines. Once a family has been disturbed the mother is quite likely to eat the pinkies, but if the disturbance occurs during or just after birth the family is easier to resettle. Newborn hoglets are difficult to hand rear, so resettle if possible, always housing a nursing mother and her litter separately from the other hedgehogs. Avoid handling and spraying because different smells will upset them. Sometimes the mother will not feed because of the disturbance. In this case the mother will have to be freed and the hoglets hand reared.

To summarise: for pinkies with a mother, try to avoid taking them into captivity. If you have to, try to resettle them together.

Hoglets more than two weeks old are most unlikely to be eaten by their mother. By this time they are miniature hedgehogs, with open eyes and hair on their tummies. They are now easy to hand rear, too.

HEDGEHOG IN YOUR GARDEN

Top: A one-day-old hedgehog already has prickles protruding from its back.

Top right: A litter of six baby hedgehogs. They are approximately two days old. Notice that the black spines are just beginning to show through the skin.

Bottom: Newborn hedgehogs are pink and do not have protruding prickles.

Pasteurised goat's milk can be used for hoglets more than two weeks old, but sterilised or dried is better. The table below gives a rough idea of the main constituents of various milks.

	Hedgehog	**Cow**	**Goat**	**Cat**
Solids (% dry matter)	21	12	13	27
Fat *	47	26	35	28
Protein *	33	26	25	40
Carbohydrates *	9	39	35	27

* as % solids.

This hedgehog is 10 days old. The eyes are still shut. Black spines are growing and so is the fur on the face. It can curl up (but not tightly).

HEDGEHOG IN YOUR GARDEN

As you can see from this table, hedgehog milk is extremely rich in fat and protein, and has a very low carbohydrate content. When you are rearing baby hedgehogs it is best to use the closest milk to that of hedgehogs. Goat's milk is therefore a much better choice than cow's milk, but kitten or puppy substitute, obtainable from pet shops, is even better for the newborn.

It is best to make up fresh bottles daily. Do not use pasteurised milk for the newborn. The milk must be sterile and therefore a powdered milk intended for kittens or puppies is most suitable.

People seeking to rehabilitate baby hedgehogs have often lost them because of infection. It is vital that all feeding utensils are sterilised before and after each feed, as for a human baby. Baby feeding bottles are ideal (after sterilisation) as containers for the milk. If pasteurised milk is used, boil it first; if powdered milk, make it up with previously boiled water.

Keep each individual hoglet's feed separate if possible, and warm it to 25°C. For the first feed, dissolve a teaspoonful of glucose into a cup of water and feed this. This will give you and the hoglet some practice. If the hoglet takes milk into its lungs it may drown or develop pneumonia.

Very young hedgehogs can take a vast amount of time to drink even 0.5ml of milk.

Guide to the amount of milk to give

Hedgehog Size	Feed
Newborn to one week	0.1-1ml
A 3-day-old hedgehog	0.5ml
(Feed every 2 hours by day and every 3 hours by night.)	
1-2 weeks (25-100g)	0.5-2ml
(Increase feeding intervals.)	
2-3 weeks (50-150g)	2-4ml
(Feed 3-4 times during the day, and wean.)	

At less than 25g weight the hoglet should be fed every two hours during the day and every three hours during the night. The feeding interval can then be increased to every three hours during the day and once in the night. Once the eyes are open (after about two weeks) they should be able to go through the night without a feed, and they should start to lap milk and eat fresh, raw, lean minced meat from a very shallow dish such as a saucer. Remember that a cold hoglet or a hoglet requiring toileting will not feed, and very young hoglets will not feed from deep dishes.

Once the hoglet has started to lap milk and eat from saucers, continue to hand feed 2-4ml milk for a further week, but also offer milk and minced meat from a saucer. Add a pinch of vitamin supplement such as SA37 daily. At three to four weeks, offer kitten/cat food and start to replace the milk with a dish of water.

Toileting

Wipe the hoglet's nose after each feed. Then take a moist tissue and tickle its genitals to stimulate it to urinate and defecate. This process is called 'toileting', and the animal could die if it is not carried out; in the normal way, its mother would do it. Faeces are greenish-yellow while the hedgehog is on a milk diet, becoming greenish-brown once it is weaned. Ensure that the hoglet is clean before replacing it in its container.

HEDGEHOG IN YOUR GARDEN

The hedgehog's eyes should look like bright buttons.

You should be able to stop toileting when the hoglet is about 18 days old and has been drinking from a dish for a few days.

Feeding on liquidised food instead of milk

Some people prefer to hand rear on liquidised food rather than milk. This is particularly useful if the hedgehog is some days old when it arrives, as is usually the case. All hedgehogs whose eyes are open can be given liquidised food instead of milk.

The following recipe is recommended, but baby beef dinners alone can be used in an emergency:

1 cup Hills Science Diet Feline Maintenance Formula*
1 jar (128g) Baby Beef Dinner (three to nine months)**

> * Dry, and available from veterinary practices and some pet shops. Other complete cat/dog foods may also be suitable.
> **Beef and Vegetable Dinners, Casseroles and Hotpots are all suitable.

Soak the Feline Formula in previously boiled water and leave for two hours in the refrigerator. Tip into a blender and add the beef dinner. Add about a cup of water and blend until the mixture is of soft ice cream consistency. Pour it into ice cube trays and store in the freezer until it is needed. After defrosting add one generous pinch of cat/dog vitamin powder. The consistency can be adjusted with baby rice or cereal and boiled water. Discard the mixture after one day.

This recipe can be used in place of milk. It is recommended when you are hand feeding for the first time as it is less likely to drown the animal. Feeding the young on liquidised food instead of milk has been practised for some years on fish eaters such as otters and seals.

At first, the hoglet is quite wakeful during the daytime. Once it starts taking substantial amounts of cat food, however, it will start to sleep during the day. Avoid handling it from now on, however great the temptation, or it could become too human-dependent to be released.

HEDGEHOG <u>IN YOUR GARDEN</u>

- At four weeks, start supplementing the diet with dried fruit and similar foods (see Chapter 6).
- At six weeks the hedgehog should have some of its permanent teeth.
- At six to eight weeks it should be self-sufficient and weigh 300-600g.

Once the hedgehog weighs about 350g and is self-sufficient, arrangements should be made for its release, provided it is not winter (November to March). A hedgehog will sometimes start gaining weight rapidly, then stop at about 300g. Most hedgehogs under 450g would have difficulty in surviving hibernation. In this case, its chance of survival would be better if it could be kept through the winter and released in April, after the late frosts. This is a general guideline as, in practice, decisions about releasing hedgehogs should always be made after studying long-term weather forecasts.

Incidentally, it is a good idea to leave dry food with hibernating hedgehogs, as they may wake up occasionally to feed.

Always weigh captive hedgehogs weekly.

CHAPTER **8**:

Releasing
HEDGEHOGS

Always release hedgehogs after dark. A hedgehog ready to be released should be in prime condition. As soon as you approach or touch it it should roll up into a ball. It should weigh over 350g (450g in November) and it should be avidly eating cat food and other foods such as sultanas that you offer it.

Baby hedgehogs are trusting and friendly. Once they become self-sufficient, however, they should become timid. This is a natural process, and returning your charge to the wild will be a serious problem if you have blunted this instinct with too much handling and hand feeding. Young hedgehogs that do not curl up the moment they are disturbed will soon be snapped up by a hungry fox!

HEDGEHOG <u>IN YOUR GARDEN</u>

As soon as the sun begins to set hedgehogs begin to wake up.

It is important to assess a hedgehog's chances of survival before releasing it. For example, a hedgehog with one back leg missing should be able to cope in the wild. It could have problems digging for food if one of its front legs were missing, however, though it could possibly manage with a stump. Assess each case individually, but consider keeping a hedgehog with one front leg missing as a pet.

A hedgehog busily foraging in the grass.

HEDGEHOG IN YOUR GARDEN

Do not release hedgehogs with patches on their backs where the spines are missing. This sometimes results from cuts, burns and disease. The hedgehog must have a complete armour of spines to protect itself. (Incidentally, the practice of cutting the spines down so that wounds can be cleaned more easily is not recommended unless it is absolutely necessary. Unless spines are completely removed they take a very long time to grow again.)

Hedgehogs that cannot be left to wander freely because of disabilities can settle down to a comfortable existence in a walled garden. Even when they are allowed the freedom of the garden they must be fed daily and provided with a suitable nesting box. They can be kept in rabbit hutches with runs, provided the wire netting is secured at ground level. As they are

Hedgehogs are wild animals that need their freedom if possible. However, if they cannot be released because of disabilities, they can settle down to a comfortable existence in a walled garden.

placid creatures, they can become quite tame. Tame hedgehogs will venture out during the daytime, especially if they can smell food!

To summarise: avoid releasing hedgehogs in November to March. Do not release them in times of drought, when the ground is too hard for them to dig. Consider keeping a hedgehog that weighs less than 450g in the middle of winter until the following spring or release in a mild spell when it reaches 450g. Do not release a hedgehog whose chance of survival is greatly lessened because of injuries.

Identification

If you want to monitor your hedgehog's progress you can leave a bead glued to one of its spines. It would not be fair to pick a brightly-coloured bead, as this would spoil the hedgehog's camouflage, lessening its chances of survival. A brown, grey or black bead would be sufficient identification to show you whether the visitor in your garden is the one you released last week. An alternative method would be to dab the spines with a dull coloured paint.

HEDGEHOG **IN YOUR GARDEN**

Where to release

Hedgehogs have some homing instinct and minds of their own, so if possible adult hedgehogs should always be released where they were found. However, this must be a place where they have access to water, plenty of ground cover and a supply of insects.

Young hedgehogs can be released directly from their rabbit hutches into the garden. They usually disperse gradually. They must, of course, be able to enter and leave the garden as they wish, and to wander around approximately 200 square metres of gardens. For a road of 60 detached houses, each with a 30m garden backing onto other gardens, release only one litter of up to six hedgehogs a year. The area may be able to support more hedgehogs than this if the people are regularly putting food out for hedgehogs, but the gardens would have to be 'hedgehog-friendly' (see Chapter 3).

After the release

Hopefully the rabbit hutch in which your hedgehog is housed prior to release is in a hedgehog-friendly garden. Feed the hedgehog until it stops returning for food. If the hedgehog decides to stay in the area, you may spot it at intervals throughout the year. It may even return to raise a family in the rabbit hutch, providing more garden hedgehogs for you to look after as necessary!

HEDGEHOG IN YOUR GARDEN

USEFUL ADDRESSES

The British Hedgehog Preservation Society
Knowbury House
Knowbury
Ludlow
Shropshire
SY8 3LQ
(Tel: 01584 890287)

CJ Wildbird Foods Limited
(suppliers of hedgehog food)
The Rea
Upton Magna
Shrewsbury
SY4 4UB
(Tel: 01743 709545)

International Union for the Conservation of Nature
rue Mauverney 28
CH-1196 Gland
SWITZERLAND

Ministry of Agriculture, Fisheries and Food (MAFF)
Whitehall Place
London
SW1A 2HH
(Tel: 0171 273 3000)

RSNC Wildlife Trusts Partnership
The Green
Witham Park
Waterside South
Lincoln
LN5 7JR
(Tel: 01522 544400)

Royal Society for the Prevention of Cruelty to Animals (RSPCA)
Causeway
Horsham
West Sussex
RH12 1HG
(Tel: 01403 264181)
National helpline (Tel: 0990 555999)

St Tiggywinkles Wildlife Hospital Trust
Aston Road
Haddenham
Buckinghamshire
HP17 8AF
(Tel: 01844 292292)

BIBLIOGRAPHY

The mammals of Britain and Europe:

BJARVALL, Anders and ULLSTROM, Staffan.
translated by Ernest Neal.
London and Sydney:Crook Helm, 1986.

Observing British and European Mammals:

BOUCHARDY, Christianand MOUTOU, Francois.
translated by Iain Bishop.
London: British Museum (Natural History), 1989.

Hedgehogs:

MORRIS, Pat. 2nd ed. London: Whittet Books, 1994.

The complete hedgehog:

STOCKER, Les. London: Chatto & Windus, 1987.

INDEX

HEDGEHOG IN YOUR GARDEN

INDEX